A Hard Choice

Written by Jennifer Beck

Illustrated by Naomi Lewis

Flying Start
to Literacy®

Contents

Chapter 1
Bushfire weather

"What's up, Dad?" Carlos asked.
Carlos's dad was looking toward the distant hills.

"I'm looking for smoke, son," he said.
"I can't see any yet but this heatwave has been going on for weeks. It's so hot outside today, and now the wind's picking up. It's bushfire weather."

Just then they heard the siren.

Carlos's family lived in a high-risk bushfire area and lots of people were trained to help the local fire brigade during the fire season. Carlos's dad was one of these volunteers.

"I need to get ready!" he said. Running back inside, his father quickly pulled on his firefighter's pants, braces and jacket, and his big, thick boots. Grabbing his helmet and keys, Carlos's dad dashed back outside.

As Carlos's dad was driving off, he shouted to Carlos and his mum, "The fire must be far away from here, and luckily the wind's blowing in the other direction. But just in case – don't forget what we've practised!"

"Okay, Dad!" called Carlos. "Good luck!"

Carlos wouldn't forget. His family had their own fire safety plan so that if a bushfire came close, they knew what to do. They had been practising their plan his whole life. If a fire was close, they had to take their evacuation kit and get to a safe place away from the fire as fast as they could.

There were also things they could do to protect their home from the bushfire, like closing all the doors and windows, turning on the sprinkler system, and filling the gutters on the roof with water.

Carlos and his mum waved as Dad sped off in his truck. At the fire station, Dad would get to drive one of the fire trucks with its large water tank and hoses.

Carlos's dad had told him about the technology that was used to find out exactly where fires were, so he knew his dad would get there quickly. Fire spotters looked out over the bush from high towers that had computerised sensors to detect smoke and flames. Radar and satellite images were used, too.

For as long as Carlos could remember, they had managed to control the local bushfires.

Chapter 2
Smoke in the air

Carlos wasn't too worried about the bushfires. After all, he thought, there was no smoke around and his dad would help put the fire out. Carlos was more interested in the hammering coming from next door.

"Can I go and see the kennel Mr Grant's made for Rusty?" he asked his mother.

Their elderly neighbour had adopted a stray pup and Carlos had become good friends with the little puppy.

"Yes, but don't go far away. I don't like the look of this weather," said his mum. "I'm going to check our sprinkler system."

"Okay," shouted Carlos, as he raced off.

"If I call you, come home straight away," his mum called after him.

Carlos found Mr Grant in his workshop, whistling along with the radio and tapping away at a nail.

"Hi, Carlos," Mr Grant said. "I just want to finish this, then I'll put my tools away."

Carlos played with Rusty and watched as Mr Grant worked. He noticed how carefully he handled each tool.

"Some of these tools were given to me by my dad," said Mr Grant. "They're like old friends. I've worked with them all my life. I wouldn't like to be parted from them."

Mr Grant looked up and smiled brightly. "Carlos," he said, "Rusty needs some exercise. How about taking him for a short walk?"

Carlos remembered what his mum had said about not going too far away. But he knew how much Rusty loved running through the trees at the edge of the bush. And he wouldn't be away long.

Carlos played a game of fetch with the excited pup, throwing the stick as far as he could and watching Rusty bolt toward it, then zigzag back happily through the trees. He laughed as the pup ran in circles, his long tongue hanging out the side of his mouth.

"I know, Rusty, it's so hot today, isn't it?" Carlos said.

Then suddenly he noticed that the wind had become hotter and stronger. And he smelled smoke. Carlos had been having so much fun that he'd forgotten all about the time!

"Oh, no!" Carlos exclaimed. "Come on, Rusty! We've got to get home!"

Chapter 3
Evacuation

"Where have you been?" his mother cried, as Carlos ran into the kitchen with Rusty. "Quick! The wind's changed, and the fire's coming this way!"

Carlos turned and looked toward the hills. On the horizon there were plumes of black smoke and a line of orange flames.

"I'm sorry, Mum – I didn't think a fire could come so quickly. I'll start hosing down the house to fill up the gutters on the roof."

"No, Carlos. I've been listening to the radio. There's been an alert. We've got to get out fast! I've already turned on the sprinkler system. Now help me load the car. You know where we keep the evacuation gear."

Carlos ran back and forth, grabbing the emergency supplies his parents had prepared. There were boxes filled with water, food, medicine, important information, a mobile phone charger, his mother's jewellery box and their favourite family photo album.

He never thought this would happen.
He couldn't believe they were abandoning their home in the path of the fire. What about all his special things in his bedroom?

"Mr Grant can't drive. I'm going to get him!" Carlos's mother shouted. "You load those blankets and clothes into the car. That's all we can take."

But Carlos was thinking of something else – the pup had disappeared!
"Rusty!" he shouted. "Where are you?"

Chapter 4
Where's Rusty?

"Carlos, get in the car now," his mum said firmly. But Carlos had already run off.

"We can't leave Rusty!" he said to himself, as he searched for the pup.

His mother caught up with him. "Carlos, this is serious," she said. "The fire is coming."

"But poor Rusty will be so scared!"
said Carlos.

"I'm sorry, but we have to go right now!"
said his mum, taking his hand and leading
him quickly back to the car. "Get in the
car, quickly! I have to get Mr Grant."

Carlos's mum hurried Mr Grant toward
their car. He was carrying an old leather
bag. It looked as if all he wanted to
save was his tools.

Carlos was so upset that he couldn't look at Mr Grant. He stared out of the car window, still searching for Rusty, as his mum quickly pulled out of the driveway.

As they sped away, he turned to Mr Grant. "How could you leave Rusty?" he asked sadly.

"Don't worry," Mr Grant whispered.
He opened the bag on his lap, and a damp
nose sniffed Carlos's hand.

"The little pup was frightened," said Mr Grant.
"I found him hiding in his new kennel.
I had to put him in my tool bag in case
he ran away."

"Rusty!" Carlos exclaimed. Then he looked up
at Mr Grant. "But your tools ..."

The old man shrugged. "Lives are more
important than things."

Chapter 5
Bushfire!

They began a frightening drive through the bush. The sky had grown dark, and smoke stung Carlos's throat and eyes. They drove through smoke and flying embers, and they could feel the heat of the bushfire.

The smoke was so thick that they could barely see the road ahead. The strong wind shook the trees loudly. Carlos sat quietly, patting Rusty. "It's okay, Rusty," he said to the whimpering pup.

But Carlos was scared, too.

Finally they reached the school oval where an emergency evacuation centre had been set up. All three of them breathed a sigh of relief – they had escaped the inferno.

I hope Dad's okay, thought Carlos.

Carlos followed his mum and Mr Grant inside where they found a group of neighbours. They were talking about trees blocking the roads, abandoned cars and homes destroyed. There was a rumour that some firefighters were in trouble.

Carlos took Rusty and sat down in the corner of the centre. The pup looked up at him, wagging his tail. "Good boy, Rusty," said Carlos, scratching the pup's ears and trying not to think about the bushfire outside.

A short time later, Carlos heard someone cry out, and he looked up to see his mother being comforted by a neighbour. She walked over to Carlos and put her arms around him.

"I have some terrible news, Carlos," she said. "The fire has swept through our street."

Carlos looked down at his lap. He knew what that meant – their house might have been lost to the bushfire.

Hours passed, with more and more people sheltering in the evacuation centre. Carlos's mum sat with him. They were both very upset and worried about Carlos's dad. Carlos didn't realise he'd fallen asleep with Rusty until he heard a man's voice. Suddenly, he remembered where he was and what had happened. He sat up quickly and looked around. Both his parents were sitting beside him. His father's face was black with ash, and he looked exhausted.

"Dad!" Carlos cried, throwing his arms around his father.

A news reporter was holding a microphone in front of them. He held it out to Carlos.

"So your father's been out fighting the fire, and you don't even know if your own home's survived. How does that feel?"

Carlos looked up at his mother and father and squeezed their hands.

"It's strange ..." he said, "but thinking about what could have happened today, I feel lucky!"

A note from the author

I've never been caught in a bushfire, and hope I never will be. However, as a child growing up on a farm in New Zealand, we did have some serious fires in the bush at the back of our farm. They were frightening to watch, even from a distance.

To research this story I read as much as I could about bushfires in Australia and North America. I was particularly interested in interviews with survivors. Through learning about their experiences I became very aware of priorities, and the difficult choices people are forced to make at times of crisis. This understanding became the inspiration for this story.